The Riddle Book

A Random House PICTUREBACK®

Roy McKie

THE Riddle

What do you call a cat
that drinks lemonade?

Library of Congress Cataloging in Publication Data: McKie, Roy. The riddle book. (A
Random House Pictureback) SUMMARY: A collection of more than thirty animal
riddles and knock knock jokes. 1. Riddles—Juvenile literature [1. Riddles. 2. Joke
books] I. Title. PN6371.5.M25 398.6 77-85237 ISBN: 0-394-83726-6 (B.C.); 0-394-
83732-0 (trade); 0-394-93732-5 (lib. bdg.)

Copyright © 1978 by Random House, Inc. All rights reserved under International and
Pan-American Copyright Conventions. Published in the United States by Random
House, Inc., New York, and simultaneously in Canada by Random House of Canada
Limited, Toronto. Manufactured in the United States of America.

31 32 33 34 35 36 37 38 39 40

Book

Random House 🏠 New York

Why does a hummingbird hum?

Because he doesn't know the words.

Where does a sheep get a haircut?

At the baa-baa shop.

How do you keep a dog off the road?
Put him in a Barking Lot.

What does a puppy say when it sits on sandpaper?   RUFF!

Why do birds fly south for the winter?

What does a penguin have that nothing else has?

Because it's too far to walk.

Baby penguins, of course.

What has four legs but can't walk?

A table.

What is worse than a centipede with sore feet?

A giraffe with a sore throat.

How does a monster count to thirteen?

On its fingers.

What is black and white and has sixteen wheels?

A zebra on roller skates.

What do you call a bull when it's sleeping?

A bulldozer.

Where do you find hippopotamuses?

It depends on where you left them.

How does a dentist examine a crocodile's teeth?

Very carefully!

When are cooks mean?

When they beat the eggs and whip the cream.

When is a farmer mean?

When he pulls the ears off the corn.

Why does a giraffe have such a long neck?

Because its head is so far from its body.

Why did the chicken cross the road?

She wanted to get to the other side.

Why do firemen wear red suspenders?

To hold up their pants.

What happens to ducks that fly upside down?

They quack up.

What do you call a crate full of ducks?

A box of quackers.

What did the porcupine say to the cactus?   Is that you, Mamma?

What did the boy octopus say to the girl octopus?

I want to hold your hand, hand, hand...

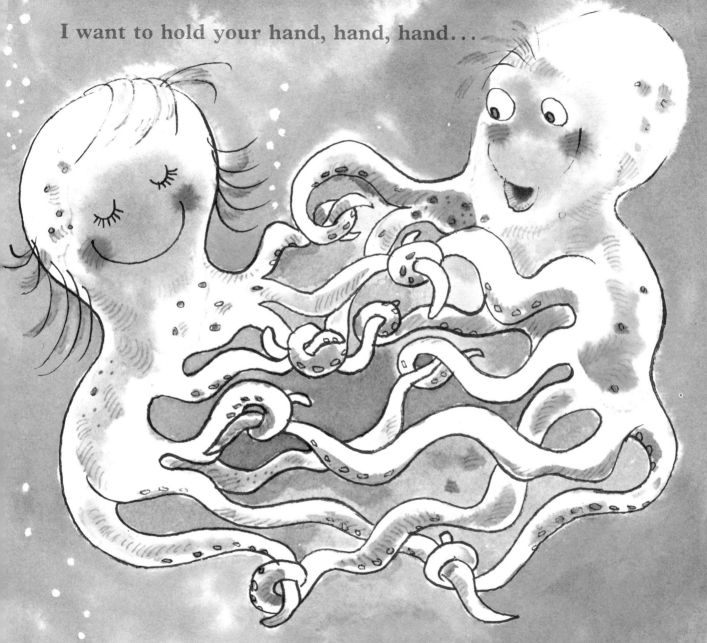

...hand, hand, hand, hand, hand.

I'd like to buy that dog, but his legs are too short.

Too short? Why? All four of them touch the ground!

What has the head of a cat,

the tail of a cat,

but is not a cat?

A kitten.

What animal can jump higher than a house?

Any animal. A house can't jump.

What time is it when an elephant sits on a park bench?

Time to fix the bench!

Where does a two-ton gorilla sit when he goes to the movies?

Anywhere he wants to!

What makes more noise than a cat meowing outside your window?

Seven cats meowing outside your window.

What dog keeps the best time?

A watch dog.